MOTHER GOOSEBERG'S BOOK OF JEWISH NURSERY RHYMES

MOTHER GOOSEBERG'S BOOK OF JEWISH NURSERY RHYMES

JEFFREY & LILA DUBINSKY

Illustrations by Dick Siegel

CITADEL PRESS
Kensington Publishing Corp.
www.kensingtonbooks.com

CITADEL PRESS books are published by

Kensington Publishing Corp.
850 Third Avenue
New York, NY 10022

Copyright © 2008 Jeff Rovin

All Kensington titles, imprints, and distributed lines are available at
special quantity discounts for bulk purchases for sales promotions,
premiums, fund-raising, educational, or institutional use. Special book
excerpts or customized printings can also be created to fit specific
needs. For details, write or phone the office of the Kensington special
sales manager: Kensington Publishing Corp., 850 Third Avenue,
New York, NY 10022, attn: Special Sales Department,
phone 1-800-221-2647.

Citadel Press and the Citadel logo are trademarks of
Kensington Publishing Corp.

First printing: July 2008

10 9 8 7 6 5 4 3 2 1

Printed in the United States of America

CIP data is available.

ISBN-13: 978-0-8065-2940-0
ISBN-10: 0-8065-2940-7

CONTENTS

Contents

CONTENTS

CONTENTS

Mother
Gooseberg's
Book of
Jewish Nursery
Rhymes

There Was an Old Woman

There was an old woman who lived
   with a Jew
Had so many dishes she didn't
   know what to do.
She gave him some cheese, and she
   gave him some meat—
It's double the work if you're living
   kashreit.

Ring Around Aunt Rosey

Ring around Aunt Rosey,
Three carats, if you're nosy.
Naches, *naches*, she found a man.

Hey, Yenta, Yenta

Hey, *yenta*, *yenta*:
"Tom Katz had a bender,
Abe Klaw took Bette to his room!"
The *kibitzer* laughed to hear such
    news,
Which Joy Tisch told at *oneg*
    shabbat.

Simple Shantzman

Simple Shantzman met a *lantsman*
Having an affair.
Said Simple Shantzman to the
    lantsman,
"Wifey doesn't care?"
Said the *lantsman* unto Shantzman,
"*Shmuck!* She is a Jewess!"
Leaned the *lantsman* close, "Besides,
The *goyim* always screw us!"

Barbara Blackman, Have You Been to Shul?

Barbara Blackman have you been
    to *shul*?
Yes, *rebbe*, yes, *rebbe*, three times
    full.
Once for a bake sale,
And once when depressed,
And once for the Sisterhood,
Where we talked and fressed.
Barbara Blackman have you been
    to prayer?
Yes, *rebbe*, sure, *rebbe*. (*Lig en drerd!*)

Hickory, Dickory, Doc

Hickory, dickory, doc.
Come fast, don't stop to knock—
I bought, full price,
A suit that's nice,
And now my wife's in shock!

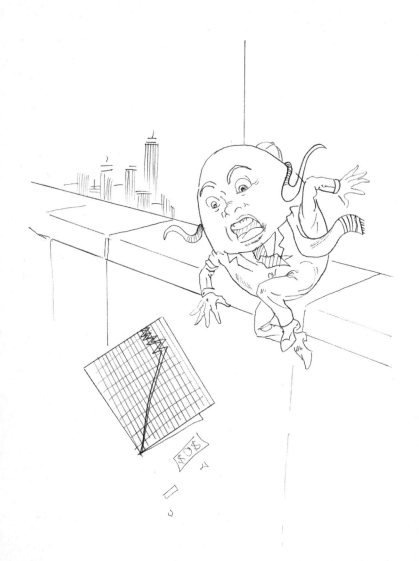

Handlen Dumpty

Handlen Dumpty traded on Wall,
Handlen Dumpty's stocks took
    a fall.
"In drerd mein gelt!" Clients made
    such a noise.
"We should have invested with
    cool-headed *goys!*"

Old Mother Bisel

Old Mother Bisel
Went to the *shisel*
To scoop her poor dog a hock.
But Herbie, her spouse,
Had finished the grouse.
Her hungry dog bit the fat *kuck*.

The Queens of Shvartze

The Queens of Shvartze,
They made some charts
Of all their autumn clothes.
No white wore they
Past Labor Day,
Lest friends turn up their nose.
A *shvartze* of Queens
Who saw the teens
Said, "Little sisters, hey—
Black blouse, black shoes,
Black skirt: black Jews—
Like Sammy Davis, they!"

Sing a Song from Mishnah

Sing a song from Mishnah,
A *brocheh* full of hope.
Three and sixty verses
Whose words can help you cope.
When you're facing *tsores*
There is no better book.
Search from "Seeds" or "Purities,"
You won't feel such a *shnook*!

Tinkle, Tinkle, Ice in Schnapps

Tinkle, tinkle, ice in *schnapps*,
Should've poured this scotch
    straight up.
Hired two guys to make me
    dough—
Jewish lightning, don't you know.
Tinkle, tinkle, ice in *schnapps*,
Who knew they were plainclothes
    cops?

Three Little Knishes

Three little knishes
Were placed on dishes
And they began to quake.
"*Oy, bubbeleh*,
See here, see here—
We do not want to bake!"
"But you are *nosh*,
For guests on Rosh
Hashanah, so, my snacks,
It's off you go
To microwave.
For sixty seconds, max."
Three little knishes
Made fervent wishes
To God, who heard their prayer.

The cook, she tripped,
And off they slipped
To only God knew where!
Three little knishes,
So fine and delicious,
Awoke on clouds above.
They smiled, but then
Were sad again:
God popped them in His stove.

Little Boy Jew

"Little Boy Jew, come blow this
  horn,
We call it a *shofar*, from ram
  it is torn."
"What do you do with the rest
  of the sheep?"
"We use some for seders, the rest
  we don't keep."
"But isn't that wasteful?" Boy Jew
  asked his dad.
"We sell that to gentiles. The
  profit's not bad."

Jews of a Shtetl

Jews of a *shtetl*
Flock to peddle
Wares from A to Z.
Rabbis get
A discount rate;
Cossacks "shop" for free.

Pop Hates a Weasel

All around the Rathausplatz square
My father chased Frau Liesl.
He said that Austrians sold him
    out—
Pop hates a weasel.

As Sy Was Going to Some Dive

As Sy was going to some dive
To find a doll, forget his wife,
He met a pimp with seven ho's
Each one of whom had little
     clothes.
Sy asked, "How much for such
     a tail?"
The man replied, "For you,
     hole sale."

PROSTATE

Ding-Dong Kvell

Ding-dong *kvell*,
Zeyde's doing well.
Prostate was big,
Swollen like a fig.
Who made it small?
Tahkeh! Dr. Ball!

Rock-a-Bye, Bubbe

Rock-a-bye, Bubbe,
In your wood chair.
When you make *greps*
The dog doesn't care.
When your wind breaks
The dog hides; he's safe.
No one can blame him—
Your wind smells like *traif*.

Old Sol Cohen

Old Sol Cohen
Liked to *daven* alone—
Just the Lord God above heard
his plea.
He prayed for a wife
Every day of his life.
When he got one, he prayed
to be free.

Georgie Porgie

Georgie Porgie, one horny guy,
Shtupps a girl and makes her sigh.
When a *goy* wants "in," she'll hiss,
"Only men who've had a *bris*!"

Jake and Jill

Jake and Jill
Bought new *tefillin*
For their rabbi, Ben.
Oy, oy vai!
The straps did fray—
Now *shin* is on his shin.

Jack Skipped Macy's

Jack skipped Macy's,
Jack skipped Saks.
On the street he bought
cheap slacks.
Jack got home and
Split the seam.
"Next time, *shmuck*, buy
Geoffrey Beene."

Little Boy Bloom

"Little Boy Bloom,"
Said Cantor Sheeson,
"Learn your *haftorah*—
A man you'll be, soon!"
"Why must I?" he whined;
His mama's eyes thinned.
A sharp *klap* she gave him.
"For gifts, foolish *kind*!"

Patty Klein, Patty Klein

Patty Klein, Patty Klein, *besuleh*,
Signed up with JDate, wants a
    fellah:
Jewish, good-looking, obedient
    to a fault.
She's thirty and single and picky—
    gevalt!

Lonnie's Bris

Lonnie's *bris* is hours away,
Folks to feed, bills to pay.
One slip of the *mohel*
And he'll be a *goil*.

Tom, Tom, the Rebbe's Son

Tom, Tom, the *rebbe*'s son,
Ate some pig upon a bun.
    His *kishkes* hurt,
    And papa did blurt,
"Now from *traif* you'll know to
    run!"

The Aunts

The aunts get off the bus in slews,
    nudjen, nudjen.
The aunts go shopping for new
    shoes, *nudjen, nudjen.*
The aunts want pumps and boots
    and flats;
Stores ask so much, you want to
    platz!
  The aunts all want deals
  On fashionable heels
From which their thick ankles will
    pour, pour, pour!

Little Ms. Stempel

Little Ms. Stempel
Sat in the temple
Eating her heart out, *oy*.
"My sister, she yachted
With people named Stoddard,
And now she's knocked up by a
goy!"

Dee Farmberg Is Not Well

Dee Farmberg is not well,
Her life has gone to hell!
Ei, ei, az och un vai!
Her story we will tell.
Dee's son, he took a *shikseh*!
They met up at a mixer!
Ei, ei, az och un vai!
Dee moaned, "That cow, I'll fix
    her!"
Too late, the two are wed!
Eloped! It hurts her head!
Ei, ei, az och un vai!
She wishes she were dead!
And now they have a child.
Her chronic fever's wild!

Ei, ei, az och un vai!
Her grandson is gentile!
But here's a secret—sssst!
That half-Jew boy she kissed.
Ei, ei, az och un vai!
His tush she can't resist!

Cobbler, Cobbler

Cobbler, cobbler, baked just right,
With a crust so fine and light.
Filled with soft, delicious prune—
Too good for my *mekhut'n*!

Ipish Pisher Yiddish Moe

Ipish pisher Yiddish Moe
Caught a cold on *shabbes*—woe!
Sniffled through the service—oh!
His – mother – told – him
Eat – chicken – soup
And – he – said – no!

Little Borscht Beet

Little borscht beet,
So red and sweet
And ready to be eaten,
All I need's
A blender, then
From "beet" you'll go to "beaten."

Three Blond Mice

Three blond mice,
Not so nice,
They make Jews run—
They're Aryan.
They all chased after a man named
     Joe,
Squeaked that they were with the
     Gestapo.
He cut them in half with a garden
     hoe.
Now three *mies* mice!

Oui, Willie Winkler

Oui, Willie Winkler,
We hate Jews;
Also Arabs, Japs, Hindus.
Don't forget Latinos
And of course the Brits.
After all, we are the French.
We hate you all to bits!

Jack Fein on Herring Dined

Jack Fein on herring dined,
His brother Saul liked lox.
Papa ate *gefilte*; they
Were fishy *alter kucks*!

One, Two: This Is a Jew!

One, two: this is a Jew!
Three, four: many *shnor*.
Five, six: some *nudniks*.
Seven, eight: most *tsedrait*.
Nine, ten: all for Zion!
Eleven, twelve: *Goy! "Elf, tvelf!"*
Thirteen, fourteen: *Shmekel shorten.*
Fifteen, sixteen: -berg, -witz,
    or -stein.
Seventeen, eighteen: In-faith dating.
Nineteen, twenty: *tsores*—plenty!

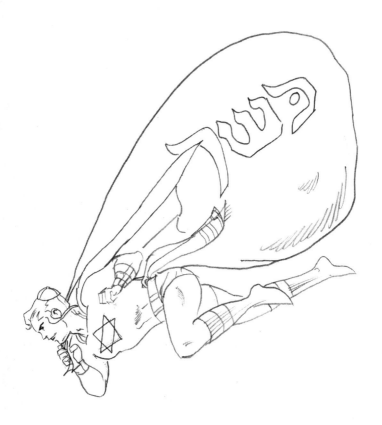

Little Jack Spitzer

Little Jack Spitzer,
On his *bar mitzver*,
Said to his guests, "God sent ya!"
He went to the door,
Gave his gifts to the poor,
And said, "Today I'm a *mensch*."

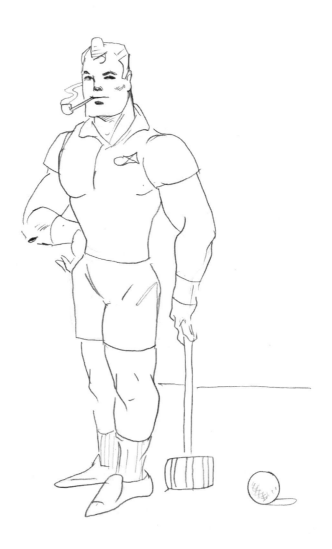

What Are Little Goys Made Of?

What are little *goys* made of?
    Polo and Yale,
    Plus weekends a-sail.
(And none of them is ever named
    Dov.)

Tsar Nick

Tsar Nick, Tsar sick.
Killed the Jews, that Slavic prick!
We wished you dead with cankered
dick—
How's the mineshaft, *nishtgutnik*?

Meshpuchas, Ten Toches

Meshpuchas, ten *toches*:
A *minyan* for *brochehs*.
What makes you *daven* so?
"We're Jews, we work
and play as one—
And where else should we go?"

This Ohmain

This *ohmain*, said in *shul*,
Said on seventeen Elul,
Followed, "Am I crazy, should I
    run away?"
This was Irving's wedding day!

This *ohmain*, said with fear,
Said as Irving's bride drew near,
Followed, "Sue is nice, whines less
    than other JAPs."
Oy! Was this a mental lapse!

This *ohmain*, said too late,
Said as Sue became his mate:
"I am to my beloved as my beloved
    is to me!"
This *ohmain* is history!

This Little Pushkeh

This little *pushkeh* is for dollars,
(This little *pushkeh* is pa's.)
This little *pushkeh* holds twenties,
(This little *pushkeh* is ma's.)
And this little *pushkeh* has
Keys to every other box!
(My car needs gas!)

Sing a Song on Succoth

Sing a song on Succoth,
I'm standing under rye,
Aravah and *lulav*;
Myrtle's in my eye,
Plus my nose is itching—
The *etrog* makes it run.
Who decided building huts
Is any kind of fun?

Hush, Little Boychik

Hush, little *boychik*, don't bother
    me.
We are Jews and can't have a
    Christmas tree.
We celebrate the Maccabees.
There's the menorah and *latkes*.
Stop this, you've got a count of
    three.
Farshtaist? Or I'll throw you across
    my knee!
And if that doesn't shut you up—
Mama's gonna give you a *luch in
    kup*!
Perhaps a *zetz* will stop your whine:
Mama's gonna *patsh* your bare
    behind.

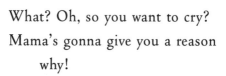

What? Oh, so you want to cry?
Mama's gonna give you a reason
    why!
No more presents; off to bed.
To think! Your grandpa was *hassid*!

For Want of a Press-on Nail

For want of a press-on nail, Fern
   decided not to play Mah-Jongg
   and stayed home.
For want of Mah-Jongg, and from
   staying home, Fern couldn't
   find the remote her husband
   misplaced after watching the
   History Channel and yet
   another show about Heydrich.
For want of the remote, Fern
   couldn't watch TV.
For want of TV, Fern decided to put
   on gloves to hide her missing
   nail, surprise hubby at the
   office, and have him take her to

lunch, which they hadn't done
since the year *gimel*—which was
also the last time they held
sexual congress.

For want of sexual congress, Fern
showed up while her husband
was *shtupping* an intern.

For want of a better explanation
than "I was trying to cure
myself of erectile dysfunction
so I could come home and
surprise you, my little
k'naidel," Fern filed for divorce.

For want of a press-on nail, a
marriage was lost!

The Dreidel That Abe Built

This is the dreidel that Abe built.
This is the child
Who sat cheering wild
And played with the dreidel that
    Abe built.
This is the *gelt*,
Of chocolate it smelt
And tickled the child
Who sat cheering wild
And played with the dreidel that
    Abe built.
This is the *nun*
He got when he spun
To win himself *gelt*—
Of chocolate it smelt

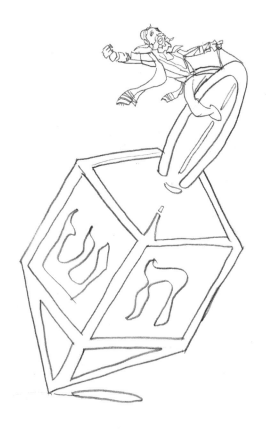

And tickled the child
Who sat cheering wild
And played with the dreidel that
    Abe built.
"This is *farpisht*!
I've won myself *nisht*!"
For naught comes from the *nun*
He got when he spun
To win himself *gelt*—
Of chocolate it smelt
And tickled the child
Who sat cheering wild
And played with the dreidel that
    Abe built.
This is a *gimel*
"I win!" *Got in himmel!*

After being *farpisht*
For at first winning *nisht*
Since naught comes from the *nun*
He got when he spun
To win himself *gelt*—
Of chocolate it smelt
And tickled the child
Who sat cheering wild
And played with the dreidel that
      Abe built.

Mary Had a Little Lamden

Mary had a little *lamden*,
Little *lamden*, little *lamden*,
Mary had a little *lamden* who
      helped with *aleph-bet*.
He followed her from *shul* one day,
Shul one day, *shul* one day,
He followed her from *shul* one day,
Which made her quite upset.
'Twixt his *payot* Mary maced,
Mary maced, Mary maced.
Then to home young Mary raced
And told her papa all.
Papa laughed, "O, Mary dear!
Mary dear, Mary dear!"
Papa laughed, "He's just a *nebbish*.
From a little push he'd fall!"

Mary sought the *lamden* out,
Lamden out, *lamden* out,
"*Oy*," she said, "I lost my head.
And *shpritzed* you with that *drek*."
The *lamden* sighed, "I meant no
      harm,
Meant no harm, meant no harm!"
The *lamden* sighed, "I just had to
      ask
About the pearls around your
      neck."
Mary grinned. "So Pa has erred,
Pa has erred, Pa has erred."
She understood: No *nebbish*, he.
That boy's a *faigelah*!

Nibble, Nibble Chazzer

Nibble, nibble *chazzer*,
My son Marv
Eats all day so he shouldn't starve.
Any food that's near, he'll carve—
The good news, *tahkeh*:
At least it's *parveh*.

Ride, Kuck Im On

Ride, *kuck im* on, to temple, and
   soon!
For this is Yom Kippur and we
   must atone.
Sha! If we're late, we will not get a
   seat.
(Plus I've got a headache from
   nothing to eat.)

There Was a Crooked Keepah

There was a crooked *keepah* sewn by
    someone half asleep,
A skullcap crooked in the sewing, so
    the seams were crooked-going.
On the head it look *farblondzhet* as
    it slowly slid, then plunged
Down to the floor—our cantor *shainer*
    looked just like a *shaigetz ainer*.